OSCAR PETERSON
Originals

2ND EDITION

Cover photo © Bill King; from the Frank Driggs © Collection

ISBN 978-0-634-09986-1

HAL•LEONARD®
CORPORATION
7777 W. BLUEMOUND RD. P.O. BOX 13819 MILWAUKEE, WI 53213

In Australia Contact:
Hal Leonard Australia Pty. Ltd.
4 Lentara Court
Cheltenham, Victoria, 3192 Australia
Email: ausadmin@halleonard.com

Visit Hal Leonard Online at
www.halleonard.com

Preface

In presenting this collection of piano pieces of mine, I have included an overview, from my view-point, of each composition. The purpose of the text that precedes each selection is a simple and direct one. It is hoped that by voicing my personal insight into some of the musical procedures utilized in each composition, and by attempting to impart them to you, the next player, this would aid you in your approach to playing and soloing on each selection.

You will encounter short manuscripted illustrations pertaining to some of my musical views about various segments of these tunes. Use them to your best advantage and feel free, of course, from an improvisational sense, to investigate and even contradict my opinions harmonically, rhythmically, and certainly from an overall interpretation.

Volume 1A represents my original compositions laid out in a pianistic style and supported by a copy of a lead sheet which will enable other players or vocalists to use as a guide. Once you have gained hands-on proficiency at playing these compositions pianistically, you should then consider going on to Volume 1B which is an expanded improvisational rendition of each of the tunes contained in Volume 1A.

In other words, Volume 1B contains a solo performance of the tunes in Volume 1A. I can only reiterate once more that it is of the utmost importance that you first give yourself a comfortable understanding of the compositions before venturing on to the improvisation version.

I sincerely hope that you will enjoy my musical thoughts put forth on the following pages.

Good luck!

O.P.

The Gentle Waltz

If we scan this composition from an overall viewpoint we will discover that it is set up in quadrants. To me, each quadrant represents a particular musical nuance. By that I mean that as we look at each four bar segment, and play each one over separately, we should be able to ascertain that each four bar segment has a personality of its own, and when put in sequence with the others, gives this Jazz waltz not only its particular shape, but also accounts for the precise direction we should take in performing it. For myself, I regard the first four bars in much the same way as an opening query that remains open-ended and becomes expanded by the second four bar melodic and harmonic content. In other words, the end of the first four bars could be perceived as having a comma and continues on into the second set of four, which contain an enlargement of the original question asked by the melodic and harmonic content of the first four bars. We can regard the first two sets of four bar phrases as being interconnected and should, perhaps, interpret them that way from a melodic standpoint. Try to envision a question mark at the end of the first eight bars, and when these two segments are played over and over we should begin to get the feeling about the question asked by the inquisitive melodic line.

The harmonic movement employed reasserts the image of the double question asked by the melodic line by not resolving totally on the F major at the end of the fourth bar, but continues on to its flatted fifth, or B minor, into another four bar segment which terminates on a D 9th chord which sits awaiting resolution.

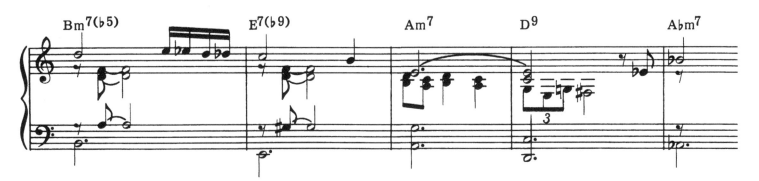

The third quadrant in our little jazz waltz commences a melodic answer to the first two questions asked in the previous two sections. By the tonality of F# minor being so far removed from the G major root of this waltz should immediately make us aware that we are on a path of finalization melodically and harmonically. At the end of the third quadrant, it tentatively rests on an A 7th still in need of the fourth quadrant in order to realize the resolution through the root key of G. The melody, by the same token, follows the harmonic direction by giving two short melodic answers to the harmonic movement in the third fourth section of four bars.

This whole first section is repeated in total, and is followed by the bridge of our waltz. The bridge is, again, segmented into four bar statements, but of a third-party kind in that they move around and differentiate from the first two sections melodically and harmonically. In our improvisational playing of the bridge we should, perhaps give consideration to making this a more definitive set of ad-lib lines, bearing in mind that the last section of our waltz is simply a repeat of the first section. I use the bridge as a form of release and definition when I solo on it so that it retains a totally different character from the rest of the piece.

In returning to the final section of the waltz, which as I said earlier, is merely a reprise of the first section, I try to return to a pensive, almost hesitant performance of the melody line, and will sometimes use a delay factor in the performance of it in order to add to its hesitancy. Incidentally, when performing this with a trio of bass, piano and guitar, it's a perfect vehicle in which to introduce the second solo voice at the bridge unexpectedly. The sound of a different solo line coupled with the change in harmonic movement and perception once again totally changes the temperament and texture of the performance.

I hope you enjoy playing "The Gentle Waltz."

The Gentle Waltz

by OSCAR PETERSON

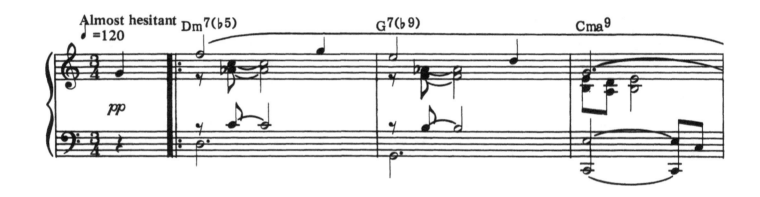

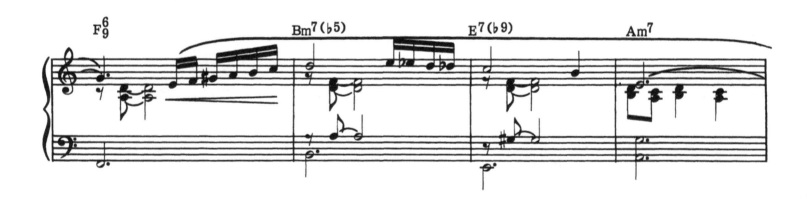

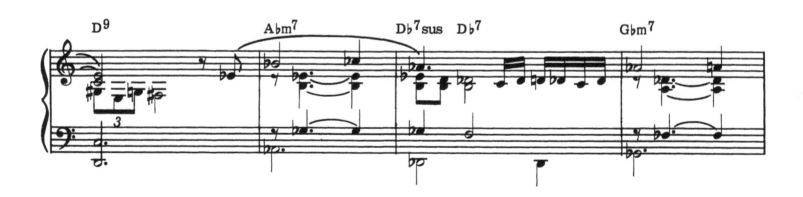

The Gentle Waltz

by OSCAR PETERSON

He Has Gone

This particular tune obviously falls in the category of being a plaintive type melody. Its strengths should lie not in the sensitive playing of the melodic octave lines, but also with the subtle underlying substitution and moving harmonies that change the overall complexion of some of the parts of the tune. For instance, in the second sixteen bar segment we substitute a C major chord in place of the A flat seventh, which alters immediately the texture and harmonic flow established in the first segment.

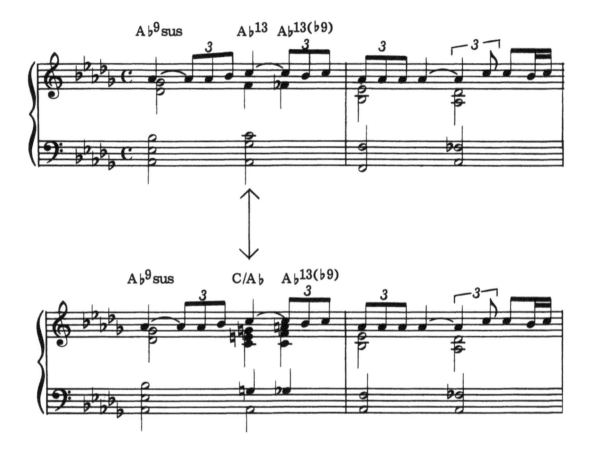

Another point I'd like to make here is that following the substitution of the C chord I prefer to use a thinner three note chord as shown so that the deviation of the C stands out more as a direct harmonic alteration, not immediately smothered by a larger four or five note chord.

The bridge should be played in a manner that makes a totally different statement in comparison to the first and last parts of the song. It should be almost a totally different segment within itself, signifying an absolute relief from the front and back sections of the song.

When I improvise on this tune with the trio, I like to have them imply, in a very soft and subtle manner, a form of double time for a couple of choruses, then I like to return to the rich harmonic, almost doleful, restatement of the tune in a simplified sense. This is a tune that I think you should approach in your own individualistic manner, considering that the melody is not horrendously involved and many, many liberties can be taken with it. The one thing that should be remembered is that it does have a sort of cry to it, and this should not be overemphasized.

As a solo piece, it affords the player many opportunities to run some diverse lines against the floating harmonies. Use your own judgement.

He Has Gone

by OSCAR PETERSON

He Has Gone

by OSCAR PETERSON

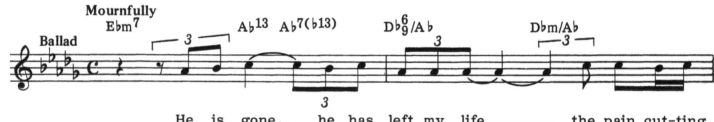

He is gone,— he has left my life,———— the pain cut-ting

like a knife,———— hurt-ing still from dusk to dawn,—— ev -'ry morn,— I'm for -

lorn,——see-ing pic-tures of his child-hood days,—— while re-mem-ber-ing the

man-y ways,——— that he taught me how to grow, and to know.

Love Ballade

The obvious first impression on looking at this music is to totally approach it from a classical point of view. This is fine in one sense, however, when I first conceived this particular piece I wanted to be able to take certain phrasing liberties which might not be considered in the classical world as the way to interpret it. My feelings remain the same to this date. There are certain parts of the selection that should be stretched, if you will, in order to add suspense from a melodic and harmonic stand-point. Case in point can be exemplified from bar thirteen to the end of bar sixteen. This entire segment should be played *ritardando* with an almost hesitant delivery of the melody, and should not resume any kind of measured tempo until bar seventeen.

There should be a noticeable pause before entering the middle segment of the piece. I use the G sharp that introduces the entry to the bridge as a totally independent pedal note allowing it to cease sounding before I go on to state the melody of the bridge.

I tend to increase the tempo somewhat in the bridge again as a deviation in concept and also to give it a totally different texture to the rest of the piece. Hesitation is used once again before entering the last segment of the composition which I usually play at the outset in an almost faltering vein, recovering to make a strong statement in both hands through the rest of the piece.

When I improvise on it I stray away from the obligato type underlying melody, preferring to use various harmonic progressions and clusters interspersed with some actual jazz figures to tie them together. After a chorus or so of this type of improvisation I return to the last part of the composition and once again enter into a pensive type of interpretation of the melody to the end.

I hope you enjoy this somewhat different jazz ballad.

Love Ballade

by OSCAR PETERSON

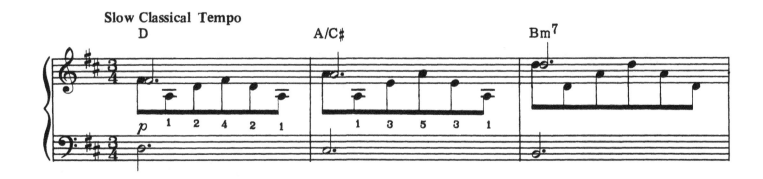

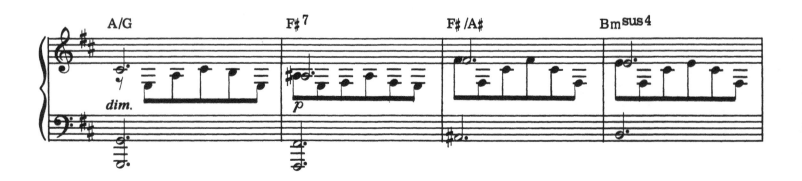

Love Ballade

by OSCAR PETERSON

Sushi

If we look at this composition from an overall viewpoint, and regard it in large context, we probably say that it comprises two major sections of twenty four bars each. The first sections ending in sort of a musical question mark by passing through the bar of D minor and coming to rest on the G seventh bar. This gives us a feeling of non-finality, in other words we perceive that there is still something to be said. The tune goes back to the initial theme for another sixteen bars, however on the final eight bar segment it resolves to its tonal base of E flat, thereby giving us the harmonic satisfaction that we seek. Looking at if from a closer viewpoint, we in reality see that it is actually a composition made up of six eight bar segments. We are free, however, to treat these in any improvisational manner we see fit.

When played as a piano solo, we should use the bass notes supplied in the original text. However, when used with the trio per se, we should relinquish the pedal G's and B flats to the bassist and use harmonic clusters that fall on the second and fourth beat as our voicing in the left hand.

The initial melody line should be strong and definitive when played, much like a front line of horns might play it, and very strong articulation should be used in the third and sixth sets of eights bars, so that the melody unmistakably takes over and gives the listener the total direction in which the piece is moving. Phrasing is most important here.

In improvising on this tune, I found that it is quite interesting to set up a phrase in the first eight, however, I would change the line from a tonal sense so that it differed melodically from the preceding eight while retaining the syncopation that was used in the first eight. When played as a trio piece, this particular configuration responds well to recurring brass type figures, which can be punctuated by the group.

Have fun with it.

Sushi

by OSCAR PETERSON

Sushi

by OSCAR PETERSON

Cakewalk

The Cakewalk is a selection that can be performed not only with a group, but because of the intermovement of the two hands, can successfully be used as a solo piece. The rollicking nature of this composition, and the rhythmic syncopation that pervades its whole melodic concept tends to make it a winner without any improvisation.

The key word in this piece is articulation. The melody itself must be played in such a way that it not only stands on its own, but also leads the left hand rhythmically when played in harmonic clusters. The idea of this tune from the first chorus out is to build, build, build. Let's go through and look at the important points of syncopation.

Any pick-up in a song is important and must be distinctively played. So this obviously applies to the D, the E flat and the F that lead into the first bar. No hesitation here! The first point of settlement is the G in the melody line, but our first major point of articulation comes with the B natural at the end of the first bar which is pushed, along with the C, D and E flat in the next bar.

Our next point of articulative importance comes in the third bar which, from the A flat to the held Bb must be played as one total phrase without segmenting it. It is most important here that the left hand stomps the F minor chord, the G diminished and the E flat chord underneath this phrase to give it the proper articulative support. It is almost like a legato phrase (R.H.) against a staccato phrase (L.H.). Both hands come to rest on the A 9-5 chord with a determined landing and then proceed on with the tune.

This type of articulative procedure continues throughout the whole tune and is the instrument used to give the composition its rhythmic gait.

If we look at the bridge we will also see the same procedure continuing except for one difference. The left hand is used to make the closing bass statement at the end of the first phrase in the bridge and should be played in such a way that it becomes a definitive point of rest.

On the second half of the bridge, after the same type of phrase is employed as it was in the opening of the bridge, the two hands begin a phrase that brings them together directionally and harmonically and to a point of finality. It is important that this whole last phrase be played with each note retaining the same density in relation to each other. In no way should the bass line override the lead or vice-versa.

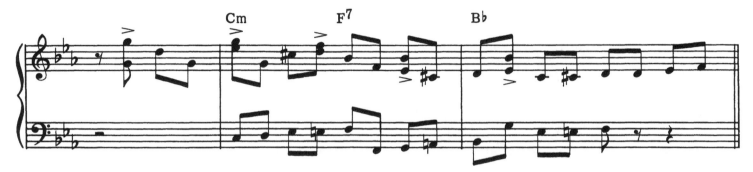

We now enter the last segment of the tune, which restates the opening melody, and continues until it runs into a two-handed phrase not unlike the one encountered at the end of the bridge. This phrase terminates with a series of harmonic gallops up the keyboard then into a finishing chord.

These segments should be played independently and should build gradually to the very end so that everyone listening expects the final E flat chord on the beginning of the bar. This, of course, doesn't happen. The ending chord is delayed by one beat, its place being taken by an unexpected rest.

Those of you that are players not experienced enough in your art to know how to play stride piano should at this point call out the rhythm section and start burning. Those of you that are that experienced and advanced in playing stride piano,

GO FOR IT!

Cakewalk

by OSCAR PETERSON

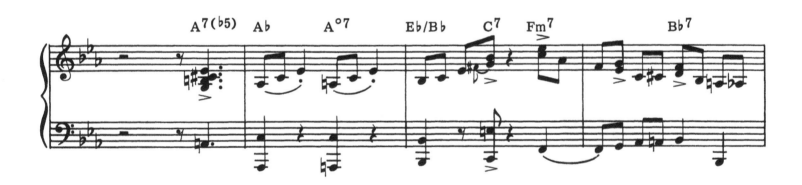

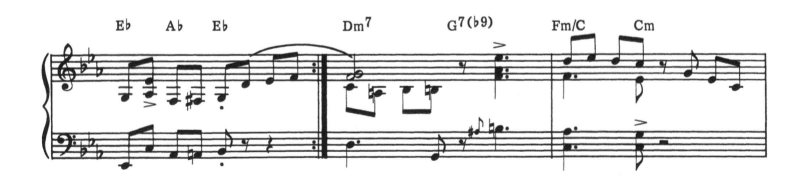

Cakewalk

by OSCAR PETERSON

OSCAR PETERSON

Biography

OSCAR PETERSON was born on August 15, 1925 in Montreal, Quebec, Canada. He studied with the gifted Hungarian classical pianist, Paul de Marky, and started his recording career with RCA in the mid-1940s. In 1950 he joined Jazz at the Philharmonic and toured until the late 1960s with that group.

Throughout this entire time, Peterson retained award-winning trios graced by distinctive players such as Ray Brown, Herb Ellis, Barney Kessel, Lewis Hayes, Sam Jones, and others. He has made numerous recordings for the various labels owned by Norman Granz from Verve through Pablo Records.

Peterson has won numerous awards, including Best Pianist for the Year by readers of *DownBeat* (for 12 years). He has won seven Grammys, and Canada honored him with the Companion of Canada in 1984, which is the highest Order obtainable by a Canadian.

Over the years, Peterson has recorded with most of the jazz greats including Dizzy Gillespie, Louis Armstrong, Ella Fitzgerald, Count Basie, Duke Ellington, and Charlie Parker.

He has, from time to time, made a point of teaching various selected students from his earlier years through the advent of the Advanced School of Contemporary Music which he founded with colleagues Ray Brown and Phil Nimmons. His interest in the music student is demonstrated by a number of primers he published.

In 1993 Peterson suffered a serious stroke which kept him from playing for two years. With a weakened left hand, he gradually returned to the scene, and the beginning of the new century found him touring and recording again.

Oscar Peterson Originals represents this phenomenal legend's desire to aid pianists that are interested in furthering their musical capabilities. This is the end to which he seems to be totally committed.